Adapt or Die:
Small Business Marketing in a Google World

The Ultimate Online Marketing Guide to Making a
Massive Difference in Your Business

Abdul S. Farooqi

Foreword by
Dr. Michael Bratland, DMD

To my Parents:

I'm forever indebted to you for all the selfless sacrifices you made for your children. Your giving attitude & insane work ethic inspired me to help as many entrepreneurs as I can

To AP, DK, UZ, NM, ST, Pagals, JK Community

Not sure if this book would exist if it weren't for your guidance, support & encouragement during the "maxima" years

CONTENTS

FOREWORD

Throughout the last decade I have been a small business owner in one of the most cost competitive professional markets- the dental industry. When I glance back at how my single practice evolved into being one of the largest dental groups in the State of Oregon, I see how our practice evolved with technology and media. The way we conduct our daily activities, the way we manage our patients, and the way we market for new patients have all transformed with the rapid and relentless improvements in technology. Without adjusting to the changing world, we would not have succeeded. Without changing, we would still be a one clinic company struggling to maintain and grow our business.

Our small business has captured a significant portion of the market share by being present in all the places where people spend a large portion of their time, such as Facebook, Google, Youtube & even other frequently visited sites using re-marketing. Thanks to Abdul & his team, we have delivered on our business goals and more importantly created awareness for our high producing dental clinics.

This is a very timely book for business owners that want more new business in this evolving world of digital media. It is particularly insightful for those business owners that have experienced little to no growth recently. This book teaches entrepreneurs how to capitalize on affordable marketing methods by leveraging digital technology. The end result is more patients, customers, and clients, which leads to more revenue.

Digital media has been one of the most effective marketing strategies in helping us grow from one to seven dental clinics in seven years. This is a feat not accomplished by many business owners because they are stuck deploying mediocre traditional marketing strategies. I find it astonishing how many dentists still spend the majority of their advertising budget on the yellow pages. After we learned how to establish a dominant presence in the digital world we spend less than when we were highly invested in TV, phone book, radio, and print. In short, we are spending less money on marketing and receiving better results.

I would highly recommend that entrepreneurs and business owners educate themselves on digital marketing or hire a competent team that can execute a sound internet marketing campaign. There a lot of companies that promote internet and digital marketing, but a very small percentage actually have the intellectual knowledge and capability to deliver on their promises. We found Abdul and his team after numerous failed attempts by companies that couldn't deliver on their promises. I am incredibly grateful to have met and contracted with Abdul. I highly endorse him and his team.

I'm delighted to introduce this book to the small business owners who are searching for creative and cutting edge techniques for growing their business. I know that you will greatly benefit from the knowledge Abdul Farooqi discloses here. Read it, and apply his techniques in your business marketing strategy. Your financial well-being could depend on it!

Dr. Michael Bratland
Owner of CrisDental (One of the Largest Dental Groups in Oregon, USA)

CHAPTER 1
A BETTER WAY TO MARKET

Why do so many businesses fail?
Because most business owners are simply insane.

When it comes to marketing their companies, most business owners do the same thing as others, however, expecting different results. This is specifically defined by Albert Einstein as "Insanity: doing the same thing over and over again and expecting something different."

We have all heard the frightening statistics that 95%, meaning 19 out of 20 business owners fail within the first five years. The ones that do survive don't really excel. They just make enough to get by.

Is it because owners are lacking in their commitment to make their business a success? Are they not motivated? Do they not put in enough hours into their business? Or rather do they lack in technical expertise for whichever service they provide?

As someone that has owned several businesses and worked with many different types of business owners, I've observed that most business owners are one of the hardest working, most ambitious and **technically superior** group of people. Most of them fail –not because of shortcomings in their effort; they fail in setting the right marketing in place to attracting their most ideal audience.

Majority of business owners simply carry out the same type of marketing that everyone else in their industry does – yet hoping for a different result than what the 95% experience - failure.

I have witnessed first-hand how setting up a marketing system that surpasses the status quo can make a business and positively transform the lifestyles of those involved and how setting up an organization with no systems can pretty much guarantee an eventual collapse for both the business and the well-being of people involved.

This is why I wrote this book, I wanted to give the smart, dedicated, hard-working dentists, lawyers, restaurateurs, contractors, realtors and all sort of small business owners & managers the most complete book on how to market their businesses in today's world of digital media - to not just survive but thrive – to completely dominate their local market and establish themselves as a leader.

The book is for you to read from cover to cover as each chapter builds upon the previous one. It will excite you with the immense possibilities that digital marketing presents for your business. It will help connect the many different moving parts in your marketing, understand the core concepts, get a better sense of direction so you can create a holistic marketing battle plan!

Create an Irresistible Offer for your Customers

If you look right now at a company that's been on the forefront of this is a company called Groupon. At one time, it was one of the fastest growing companies ever. What they do is, every single day they pick a company to feature and create an irresistible offer with that company. For example, let's say, it's a laser hair removal service. Something the business will usually sell for $750, they'd sell for $99, and this special offer on Groupon goes to 100,000s of people in the city. During that one day, because of that insane offer, you might sell a hundred, or thousands, or more of this service because you created an incredible, irresistible offer.

This is one of the most important things in your business. An irresistible offer, if you create it correctly will literally catapult the rest of your business forever. Display that offer on your site's landing page, and it'll massively increase your lead conversion numbers.

The best story of the "irresistible offer" is of Domino's Pizza. The pizzeria was originally a little restaurant called Dominic's. Two brothers bought the restaurant and tried to run it and didn't have very much success with it. One of the brothers actually sold back his half of Dominic's for a Volkswagen. If you are looking at the pizza business, this is by far one the most hyper competitive industry in all of restaurant world. If you look into the yellow pages and look at the restaurant section, there's every restaurant in the city in the restaurant section except for pizza.

Pizza has its own section in the phone book just for pizza because there are so many competitors in that industry, so it's by far the most aggressive, most difficult industry out there. They came in as a no-name company, they went in against all other pizza places including Pizza Hut which was the number one Pizza place in the world at the time, and they came and they created an irresistible offer. A simple & relevant offer. It was *"hot fresh pizza delivered in thirty minutes or it is free"*. That was the irresistible offer.

Now we may say that it's not a big a deal, but at the time people were used to having slow delivery, pizza would be cold or by the time it got there the basketball game would be over. It was an irresistible offer that literally changed the way business was done, forever. Domino's went from being an unknown pizza place to becoming the largest chain in the world, beating out even Pizza Hut because of their irresistible offer.

When you have an irresistible offer, that is really the catalyst to any business. The first thing we need to do is, we need to create a mouthwatering offer for your service & display it on the business website. This is something that is going to get somebody in the front door. One great example, was one guy doing door-to-door lawn service and exploding his business literally overnight. All the lawn mowing companies were usually giving the offer of, *give us a call, and we will come give u a free quote for mowing your lawn.*

That was the offer everyone was giving.

He thought, "How can I make an irresistible offer that's so good that everyone will have to take advantage of it? He said what if we mow the people's lawns for free? He said instead of charging, we will mow their lawn for free and if we actually mow their lawn, they will probably want to call us. We'll then get them on a monthly payment plan and make money in the long run.

Okay, we are going to give away a free lawn mow. We are going to put up this ad that basically says, *free lawn-mowing.* They ran it on Craigslist, ran it on other sites, and what happened was interesting. Despite all the different lawn mowing companies competing for attention, people started gravitating to his offer because of its irresistible nature.

Too often when we look advertising out there, in the top portion of the website where the irresistible offer should be, it says, "we've been around since 1980s" or, "we are out on the corner of MainStreet and Broadway", they are focusing on themselves, and stroking their ego.

They are supposed to be focusing on the customer, the customer, the customer. So make sure that your offer is focused on the customer. Again, if you're confused on how to create an offer, go to *groupon.com,* start looking at all offers that they are running, and you're going to see which offers are irresistible. The ones that have a hundred, a thousand, five thousand sales in a day are irresistible offers. The ones that make one or two sales in a day, are not irresistible offers.

Figure out how you can create irresistible offers in your business.

Build the Value Ladder

I'll use the lawn mowing business as an example to explain this concept. I knew of a lawn company that used this concept very effectively to completely dominate their competition. They started out by offering lawn mowing services for free. What's interesting is after they would come and mow the person's lawn for free, and while the person is mowing the lawn, they look around and observe all the things that would be lacking in the owner's yard.

They notice the grass is dryer because the sprinklers are not working, or there is weeds are taking over; Maybe they need some fertilizer on the lawn, some aeration, and they start up-selling these other services and start making a lot of money as a company, not just mowing lawns but on all the other services, they sold on the backend; and so that leads me to **the concept of the Value Ladder.**

Now let me kind of tell you a funny story about my life so that you will see the power in a Value Ladder. You kind of just saw it in the lawn mowing company, but here's dental example. There is a Dental Client that does one dollar new patient exam. For a dollar, patients come in; they do a consult, they do an exam, they x-ray, you pay a dollar to come in the first time. For a new patient, that sounds great, they love it and get their teeth done.

At the clinic, they look at the teeth and during the consultation they ask questions like, *"Hey Patient X, I'm curious, did you used to wear a retainer or used to wear braces?* "Well I can tell, because your teeth are starting to shift again".*

> Patient: Are you serious? My teeth are shifting?
> Doctor: *Yeah, there are starting to shift again, I just noticed them, I just wanted to see if you use to wear braces.*
> Patient: Yeah, I did but I don't want my teeth to shift back again, is there anything I can do?
> Doctor: *Well, if you want we can create a retainer for you, and then at night you can wear this retainer and it will keep your teeth in spot to prevent shifting.*
> Patient: Yes, please build me that retainer, I don't care how much it cost, just build it.

Dentist builds the retainer and makes $2,000 - $3,000 dollars from a $1 irresistible offer. Then he is doing his teeth some more and he says, *"Hey Patient X, I was curious, are you a smoker or do you drink coffee?* He says, "No, I don't smoke or drink coffee, why do you ask that?" "*Well your teeth are kind of yellow, I was just curious if you smoked or drink coffee, that is usually why people have yellow teeth"...* and then also goes on to sell another solution..

If the Patient has a wife or friends, they may also be told to go in for a one dollar trial, and leaving also with retainer, invisalign, teeth whitening kit or more. A one dollar client can end up spending close to ten thousand dollars from a simple trial, but they don't care because they are receiving value in the value ladder, and NOT being forced to buy anything, because your services are aligning with your moral obligation towards the patient.

CHAPTER 2
YOUR WEBSITE: NOT JUST A PRETTY FACE

The goal is to have a site that's actually generating leads and making you money. Do not fall in the trap of making a beautiful brochure website, I promise you there are companies out there that can make a beautiful website but never generate business. Websites that generate patients, leads and make money give your business prosperity, that's what you need.

As a high school student, I was taught to use the acronym K.I.S.S when writing papers. It stands for "Keep It Simple Stupid." When designing a website the same mantra should be practiced. Websites do not have to have a lot of bells and whistles in order to attract customers. In fact, many customers will be turned off by a website that has this. When browsing the Internet, customers do not want to spend a lot of time on a website if it does not have the information they need. They will often go to the website, obtain the information they are looking for, and close out the window. Fancy websites can be overwhelming to customers.

Be sure to only include the most important information on the website. You may need to narrow this down to a few key points. People browsing the Internet do not have time to read an essay on a website. As stated earlier, they are looking for certain information. If said information seems to be unattainable, they are not likely to stay on your webpage. They will move on to another page where the information is more readily available.

It is easy to add content, photos, graphs, etc. to websites that you think are important. It is nice to have a website that plays music in the background or maybe has a slideshow on every page. Instead, think to yourself, is all of this really necessary? Do my customers really care about music? Are they really going to read the graphs? Does any of this help in selling the product or does it scare customers away? Keep in mind to K.I.S.S. and remove anything that is not pertinent to selling the product. After all, isn't having a website supposed to lead to making money in one fashion or another?

Here are some tips to help you in designing your website and making sure that you keep it simple.

Design is a way for you to communicate with your customers. All of those graphs and charts should be discarded before they even make it onto the webpage. Humans are not naturally made to crunch numbers. On the contrary, they need to see visuals. The best way to represent your product is to present it in photographs or other visual elements. The more visuals you can add, and the less words, the better off your website will be.

People have differing opinions on what constitutes as a good design. It is often subjective. This means you cannot always meet the need of every person who visits your webpage. No matter how you do it, you have the chance of someone not liking your page. It is the nature of the beast. You know what they say, "Everyone is a critic." This is not to say that a page will never look appealing. It is just to say that, to reach the optimal amount of people, your webpage design should be aesthetically pleasing. Simply put, it should be pleasing to the eye. If the colors are too bright, or the pattern is hard to read over, customers will move on to another page.

People should have an emotional connection to your website. If they can connect to your website on an emotional level, they are more adept to use your website for future references. The human mind is set-up to connect on an emotional level. It is natural. Use this knowledge and wiring to your advantage. We are not saying that you have to make people cry when they are viewing your website. Just make the website personable so people feel they are connected in some way. This can be as easy as having a comment box that can be easily found. Normally we would not suggest making money off of people's emotions. However, you have to play to your strengths.

No matter what you may think, the design of the website is important. When your website has a good design, it will not go unnoticed. People will keep coming back. They will remember how easy your site was to navigate. They will remember, if not consciously, how they felt when they viewed your website. This means you will be able to see your products at a higher cost because there will be a high demand. It is simply economics of supply and demand.

Great first impression. This is something we all want to make. It is part of human nature. Did you know that your website is often the first contact a customer will make with your business? After doing research through search engines, such as Google, they will come across your website. This means you need to leave a lasting impression. Your website needs to stick out so they remember it later. If they do not remember it, they should at least feel the need to bookmark it so they are able to visit it later.

Keep your target audience in mind. Every website has a group of people their content is targeted towards. When designing your page keep them in mind. You need to make it known, without words, who you are targeting. For example, if you are targeted women ages 17-24, feminine colors can be used with simple patterns such a floral and/or lace. For older women you can use feminine colors but have no or limited patterns. This will comfort them in knowing that the website will be a good resource in helping them achieve their specific goal.

Use the human mind to your advantage and form an emotional connection with potential customers. They will probably not realize they are having an emotional connection because it will be subconsciously. Make sure to only include the pertinent information. Customers are not going to spend a lot of time on your website if it is hard to navigate.

First and foremost, keep it simple!

CHAPTER 3
GET PAID TRAFFIC

AdWords Basics

The first thing we are going to talk about and what we are going to do is start at a high level and then we are going to get into the nitty-gritty details. The first thing is the pyramid of success, the very top thing that the pyramid has is **measure** and you cannot improve what is not being measured.

The next thing is **analyze** and it is basically crunching the numbers to find what is working and what is not.

The last part is **optimize** and is basically scale what is working or decrease what is not.

Measure is at the top because it is most important, what can be measured and where visitors are located? Time of day, day of the week, what network the traffic is coming from. Important actions like conversions and the exact words that your visitors type into Google.

Mobile Traffic

There are a couple common flaws that business owners typically have when advertising. They can be advertising to mobile but their mobile site is nonexistent. One example of that could be, you click on their mobile Ad, costing them money, pull their mobile site and try to click on their phone number and the tap functionality to call the number doesn't work. It is going to hurt conversions.

Landing Page Experience

Another thing is that the website simply takes too long to load or the click leads nowhere. Believe it or not you can find websites that are advertising in Google Adwords, spending money where you go and click on their sites and it is actually not loading. It doesn't take a rocket scientist to know that it is a bad thing.

Set Up Remarketing

Remarketing are those annoying ads which seem to follow you around the web, reminding you of that dental clinic's website you looked at last week & have been delaying going to. They may be annoying, but they convert! Google has provided step by step instructions on how to set up your remarketing tag.

Once you have done this, every visitor to your site will be 'tagged' and you can create rules to serve tailored ads just to them. For instance, you can serve ads to visitors who have reached the checkout page of your website but did not choose to buy. Remarketing is a highly effective marketing technique, so you want to be building your list as soon as you start generating traffic through Adwords.

SCIENCE! What is the Rarest Precious Metal?

Adword Extensions

Another thing is a lack of the bells and whistles for adwords. Three of the biggest ones are sitelinks, location pin and call extensions (see image).

Site links is when you can see links to other pages within the sites and the call extension is when you see the phone number in the ad. Having these extensions makes your advertisement cover more space in the search results and therefore increases your ad's likelihood of getting clicked.

Incorporating Negative Keywords

Advertising to non-relevant keywords is one of that largest holes most business owner's advertising strategies. When advertising for a particular keyword, let's say "dental", the ad may show up for terms that include that word but will not drive new business, such as "dental jobs", "dental chairs for sale", "dentist career", "life of a dental student". You don't want to be spending money to get clicks from people that won't walk into your business. Incorporating for negative keywords within your Google Adword campaign combats that.

The following is a fantastic tactic I use for every PPC client I have ever worked with. Negative keywords are so important because you don't want your ad to show for non-relevant keywords. Here's what you do once you go to www.google.com. Start typing in your main keyword. For this example, we will
assume you have dental clinic in california. Look what happens when you begin to type "dental clinic"

Google   dental clinic

dental clinic **in jurong west**
dental clinic **names**
dental clinic **hougang**
dental clinic **website**

About 49,000,000 results (0.77 seconds)

Straight away we have identified multiple negative keywords. You don't work in "jurong west", you're not looking for "dental clinic names", "hougang" or a "dental clinic website". Each of these could be added as a negative keyword as you don't want to show your ad to people searching for any of these things. Go through the whole alphabet like this for all your main keywords and you will soon have a comprehensive negative keyword list.

Dimensions & Segments

In the Adwords platform, you have two best friends that are called dimensions and segments and that is where you can find them, I have showing this a couple of people and it has been huge for them.

Within the dimensions tab, you can see: time, days of the week, hour of the day, searched terms, distance, user location, geographic areas, destination URLs. Small business owners must understand that ad and keywords perform differently at different times of day and that makes sense, that at 3 o'clock in the morning things are going to work differently than at 3pm.

If you are using multiple landing pages, you can see exactly how they are performing differently. This is like I said one of your best friends to mention and then segment. They are very similar and you can get out some of the same information, with segment what it does

The most important thing with each marketing campaign is MEASURE, which is at the top of the pyramid. Measure is all about conversion tracking, if you are not tracking conversions, we call it flying blind.

What can you track? You can track form submissions, phone calls, online sales. Ensure that conversions are being tracked properly. What business owners need to do is to put them on what you call the thank you page or confirmation page. So you generate a conversion code and then you place it on the page after the action.

I was talking to somebody that was spending $100,000 per month but they weren't actually tracking conversions properly, there was a two page step with their purchasing process and they put the conversion code on page 1 of the checkout as well as the 2nd page, resulting in conversions being counted incorrectly. They immediately adjusted their marketing budget after they learned they were getting must lower conversions.

Assign Value for Each Action – Conversion tracking allows you to assign a value to the different conversion actions. What is the value of a phone call, what is the value of a sale? With an E-commerce site it is really easy because how much was that sale, but some of the other things I like what is the value of somebody submitting a contact form on your website. Basically what you want to do is then run the math and say 10 people fill out the contact form, what actually resulted in that? We got one sale from that but what was the value of that sale.

The important thing about the conversion tracking is to not cloud your data with less important conversions. For example, when you measure the value of sales versus phone calls you want to make sure that what you are seeing in there are things that you want to take action on. Let's say if you are not making any money on the contact form then you might not want to have it in there, you don't want to cloud your data. Recently, Google has added the phone call tracking in United States so numbers are another trackable metric with adwords.

Adword Campaign Structure

Structure is another big problem with most accounts. I see a lot of business owners piling tonnes of keywords, a couple of ads, under one campaign or one ad group. This results in an inefficient account. A good account structure looks like you got a couple campaigns that should be categories, several ad groups underneath those campaigns and then the ad groups should have a couple of ads that are split testing and anywhere from 5 to 25 keywords. You want to make sure that the ads are very relevant to those keywords. Those are good campaign settings.

Location Specification

Location allows you to advertise exactly where you want. Not just by cities or countries, but also by postal codes & by distance around a specified location. When going through these settings, business owners need to be careful of an option between "people searching for… about my targeted location" and "People in my targeted location".

For example, we had a client that was having a big problem that was located in Surrey, British Columbia, Canada but they were getting a lot of clicks from Surrey, UK. So how does Google know is they are searching for Surrey in British Columbia, Canada or Surrey in the UK? These are the settings that can really trip you up and they are tripping up many, so I recommend setting it up to "people in my targeted location".

⊟ Location options (advanced)

Target ⑦ ⦿ People in, searching for or viewing pages about my targeted location (recommended) ⑦
  ○ People in my targeted location ⑦ ◀━━ choose this one
  ○ People searching for or viewing pages about my targeted location ⑦

Exclude ⑦ ⦿ People in, searching for or viewing pages about my excluded location (recommended) ⑦
  ○ People in my excluded location ⑦

That means that if somebody is physically located in Florida that is how you are going to be able to target them, not if people are viewing pages about Florida, somebody might want to take a trip there, you don't necessarily want to advertise to those people.

Once again, these settings that Google presents can help you make your marketing campaigns more profitable. Once you are tracking your clicks & conversions, you can review performance of different your geographic regions using the dimensions or settings tab, you can look at, states, city and ZIP Code and analyze whether visitors from different regions perform differently.

You can then reduce the bids or exclude graphical locations with a high cost for conversion.

Time Optimization
You can set your AdWords campaigns for certain time of day and certain days of the week and if you are going to have underperforming times of day, as well as days of

week, you can have your click bids adjusted for that. You want to exclude your ad from showing at all in the middle of the night when your staff is not there answering the phone? You can stop the ads completely or adjust the bid down by a certain % so you don't waste money. Here is an example of that. Between midnight to 6 AM, a dental clinic spends $500 in a week yet receive zero connected calls or emails.

Knowing that information, you can stop advertising during that time of the day and that budget can be allocated towards more production hours. Once again, you don't have to shut it off 100% you can even reduce the bid by 50% or any given percentage.

Optimizing for Mobile Devices

Are your ads triggering on mobile devices? This is something you can look at and if so is the website mobile friendly, or does the average visitor have to pinch the screen or squint the eyes to read. According to Google, mobile searches are expected to exceed desktop by 2016.

Once the website is mobile friendly, you look at how conversions compare on mobile versus desktop and then have mobile bids adjusted accordingly.

Advertising Networks on Adwords:

There are 3 different networks on Adwords, which are Google search, search partners and the displayed network. By default Google wants you to select 'Search Network with Display Select'. It's top of the list

and they call it the 'best opportunity to reach the most customers'. Which sounds good on paper but is is difficult for most small business owners to master.

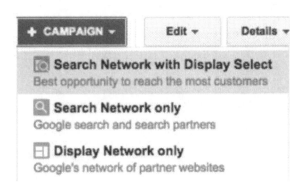

If you do decide to use the search partner option, you can again use segment tab to measure how effective the search partners have been. If you've spent money but with zero conversions, you can turn that off.

Keyword Match Types

There are 4 match types on Google and those are Broad, Modified Broad, Phrase & Exact. You've got to be careful of broad match, the ones that are preferred are modified broad, phrase and exact and you should have a mix of those match types. Start out with broad match type, as you learn which search types are bringing you the most amount of clicks, you can start targeting those with phrase or exact match types.

Match type	Special symbol	Example keyword	Ads may show on searches that	Example searches
Broad match	none	women's hats	include misspellings, synonyms, related searches, and other relevant variations	buy ladies hats
Broad match modifier	+keyword	+women's +hats	contain the modified term (or close variations, but not synonyms), in any order	hats for women
Phrase match	"keyword"	"women's hats"	are a phrase, and close variations of that phrase	buy women's hats
Exact match	[keyword]	[women's hats]	are an exact term and close variations of that exact term	women's hats
Negative match	-keyword	-women	are searches without the term	baseball hats

How do you determine if a term in unprofitable? Let's say, after all expenses, you profit $1000 per sale. If Cost Per Acquisition (CPA) > $1000, you'll fall into a loss. You want to look for the bleeders with zero or few conversions spending more than your "Cost per Acquisition" threshold. What we commonly see in an account is that all the keywords will be broad and typically, Adwords costs could be reduced by simply changing the match types for some of the most common keywords in the campaign – provided they are bringing conversions profitably. A more specific match type leads to a higher Quality Score by Google Adwords, and that has a corresponding impact on your cost.

Interested in knowing what impact match types have to your advertising costs? You can determine this by clicking the segment button while on the "Keyword" tab within your Adwords account.

Keywords that are underneath threshold (Profit Per Sale – CPA = 0) can be added as a negative keyword. The negative words tell Google I don't want my ads to be displayed for that and those also have match types.

Trimming the Broad Fat

Search terms are the actual phrases that people type on Google and most people think that the words you see on the far left column in the "keyword" tab are the keywords that you are advertising. It is really not that because Google likes to be broad with their default broad option and that Match Type can trigger all sorts of keywords. The "search terms" button under the Dimensions tab or click "Details" & select "search terms" under the "Keywords" Tab. This includes the actual keywords and this is a big area that can trim a lot of fat.

When you see a lot of broad match you want to pay very close attention to the type of clicks it's generating. A lot of these clicks will be irrelevant, so you'll want to move those into negative keywords or move the relevant ones into **modified broad**, **phrase** or **exact** match.

Typically, broad match is too broad; exact and phrase match can be too low volume. Go for modified broad match for the best mix of volume and targeting. This means using + before each word, meaning that the word has to appear for your ad to be shown.

Google Ads Optimization

Let's talk about ads. The keywords should be added into the ad headline itself because it gets bolded once someone inserts that word into the search and that in turn increases the clicks through rate (CTR). In your ad, you want to highlight benefits and features, generally in the descriptions and you want to try and grab the attention, use urgency, scarcity, a call to action and another thing you want to do is try testing extended headlines. You can try doing that by having a period or punctuation at the end of the description line 1 and what it actually does is moves the description up to the headline. So instead of just 25 characters it now becomes 25+35 characters.

Characteristics of a Great AdWords Ad:

San Diego Cash For Cars - ████ UsedCars.com — **Extended Headline**

Ad ████ rs.com/Cash-For-Cars-SD ▼ +1 800-████ — **Great Offer**

We Buy Cars Up To $100,000 Fast. Cash For Cars Offers in San Diego

Free Car Appraisals · We Do All DMV Paperwork — **Extensions**

Submit Car Free   We Come To You

We Pay $50 to $100,000   Sell Your Car

Ad extensions

One of the most important things pertaining Google Ads are Sitelinks and Call Extensions. Site links is when you see additional links in the ad and the example that I like to use for that. Let's say you are looking for a restaurant and you search on that restaurant's name.

What are you probably looking for? Direction, menu, to book a reservation, hours, reviews and that is what you are able to do with the site links. You can show those things and they can dive right into the site, right to where they really want to go, those increase the click through rate. The call extension is when you show the person's phone number and that person dials you directly rather than browsing through the website. For most local business owners, the conversion ratio with mobile call extension ads is much higher. If they are not using call extensions, they are leaving a lot of income on the table.

The main thing is just knowing where to look and it is mainly dimensions and segments, location extension that shows address, seller ratings if you want to show the stars in the ad. There is a misconception that you can only get reputation stars for e-commerce sites but you can get it for local businesses as well but the resources you want to use for that is not free; It's called trust pilot, which is a third-party service that will contact your customers and requests reviews from them and once you get about 30 reviews that is when they start showing up in the ads and once again that helps increase the click through rate, it helps set you apart from the competition.

Another thing is the **review extension**, it shows third-party reviews anybody has seen this one? It is fairly newer the big thing about that is they don't accept the different sources. But some of the sources you can include with which a lot of people are familiar with and maybe have is the BBB so you can do BBB A+ rated a lot of them will disapprove but BBB, Inc. any like official type sources you can have on there, call ad extension that is a really new one and what you can do there is, it is similar to site link but they are not actual links but you call out things like free teeth whitening and limited time offers things of that nature.

That is where you find ad extensions, there is a little tab right there ad extension and there are the different kinds site links, locations, call, app, review call out, so you just going there and see if they are using them and if they are using them you can see how they are performing as well as but once again these are things that these are like feathers in your cap, when you are looking at an account if they don't have these things that these are easy things that you can do to improve the results. Once again ad extensions are proven to increase the click through rate, help improve quality score they are great way to get attention and they checked at each campaign contains site links, called extensions and location extensions - which is primarily made for local businesses because for example, e-commerce site don't tend to have a phone number in their ad even though it has been proven to increase the click through rate.

Landing Pages

The main thing you want to ensure is that you have the phone number prominently in the header - that is really important. Most businesses want phone calls. If the number is not very prominent then how are visitors going to call. For mobile devices, the number should be clickable. You need to have a clear call to action and not too much going on. Call to Action such as, schedule an appointment, get a free quote, things like that and you want to have an irresistible offer.

What offer can you put out there that is just going to compel them and pick up the phone and call you right now, especially when've loaded your offer with scarcity and urgency. Those two compound that irresistible offer to make them take action now.

You want to make sure that the website loads quickly - under two seconds basically is what we want to look at. Once again, if we say we are advertising to mobile and you don't have a mobile friendly website then it is easy to get a mobile friendly website to improve your results. The other thing is that if you are not advertising to mobile due to some misconception that there's not that much traffic on mobile or its important then look into studies published by Google that reveal that the number of mobile searches is going to overtake the number of desktop by next year. I am sure in some industries it probably already has.

In fact, Google's keyword planner tool now compares the traffic between mobile and desktop and in most industries, atleast 50% of the searches were actually happening on mobile. Up from 0%, just a few years ago. You've got to have a mobile site. In the past, it might have been a nice to have, however, now it is a must have.

Key Performance Indicators

Let's talk about some KPI's, key performance indicators. Click through rate (CTR) is one of the most important KPI because ad clicks are conversions to Google every time somebody clicks on your ad they make money and they like that, they like making money and the way that you get the click through rate is that you divide clicks by impressions and generally it will be something like 1%, 2% something like that but the higher the better and it is the most important metric in determining quality score.

The Quality Score

This is Google's secret sauce, which is how they maintain economic balance of the auction because AdWords is an auction model and it basically rewards better advertisers, so business owners that have the best, highest converting relevant ads and landing pages get the highest quality scores.

How do you find out your quality score? This is something that is initially hidden in your google dashboard. You have to go and change your column settings to see it because they are so many different things that you can show, tons of columns and they don't just show them all by default.

On the "keywords" tab, you can unhide this key data by clicking column>modify column>attributes and adding "Quality Score" into the list of columns that are shown.

Modify columns

Select metrics

Attributes	»		Add all columns
Performance	»	Campaign type	Add
Bid simulator	»	Campaign subtype	Add
Google Analytics	»	Labels	Add
Competitive metrics	»	Bid strategy	Add
		Bid strategy type	Add
		Landing page	Add
		Tracking template	Add
		Custom parameter	Add
		Qual. score	Added
		Est. first page bid	Add

When somebody searches on a keyword they are clicking on that ad. The quality score is from 1 to 10 and usually seven or above is great. Once again, if in your account you see a bunch of threes then you know there is an opportunity to save money or generate a greater ROI.

Increase in quality score gets you a higher average ad position and a lower cost per click. A lower quality score may result in a decrease in the % of times you ad is shows when someone searches for a relevant term, called the impression share. By improving that quality score, your Google Ad will show up more, so that will bring more traffic.

Once again, the main way to increase the quality score is to optimize landing page experience, increase & the click through rate.

What increases the click through rate? Having keyword relevant ads, having a compelling offer, the urgency, the scarcity, using the ad extensions, the site links all of these things have been proven to increase the click through rate and that is how you optimize the quality score.

Regarding quality score, what I like to look for is that at least 30% of keywords have a quality score of seven or above – this is typically what an optimized campaign looks like on a high level.

The lower the average, the more costly the clicks, what you want to do is start with keywords that have the most impressions and we call this impression weighted, the impressions and let's say you have two keywords they both have a quality score of three, one has 1000 impressions, the other has 100 impressions you want to focus on the keyword with 1000 impression first because that is the one that is dragging the account down the most.

Summary

AdWords and Pay-Per-Click is an area that confuses people and it seems like a lot, but once again, basic knowledge in this area or having a marketing consultant is a must. By following the principles mentioned in this chapter, you can get miles ahead of your local business competitors and dominate your market!

CHAPTER 4
GET ORGANIC TRAFFIC WITH SEO

So what is SEO?

Search Engine Optimization is the process of influencing natural search results so that your website obtains a high-rank for certain search phrases.

SEO is not:

1. *Not about buying keywords.*

2. *Not telling Google where we want to be ranked*

3. *Not a very fast process*

4. *Not shady*

5. *Not incredibly difficult*

This is not about calling up Google and asking them to place your website number 1. This is not a very fast process. It's not a shady process. The industry has a reputation of being shady and shady people in it, but I promise you it's not, and there's good people that do it. And it's not incredible difficult either. That's the counter intuitive piece of this. Once you get the principles behind it, it's actually easy.

Let's talk about the Oracle of SEO, Matt Cutts. He is the head of the web spam team at Google. He's the equivalent of Ben Bernanke from the Federal Reserve. What he says, everyone listens, and they dissect what he says word for word. What did he mean when he said this? The whole industry sort of listens to what he said, and then makes an assumption on how the search algorithm has shifted.

Here's some advice from the Matt Cutts about SEO:

SEO stands for Search Engine Optimization, and essentially just means trying to make sure that your pages are well represented within search engines. And there's plenty, an enormous amount of stuff that you can do, as a search engine optimizer.

Good Practices:

You can do things like making sure that your pages are crawlable. You want them to be accessible, people to be able to find them, just by clicking on links on the website. And in the same way, search engine

48

can find them, just by clicking on links. You want to make sure; that people use the right keywords. If you're using industry jargon or lingo, that not everybody else uses. Then a good SEO can help you find out which keywords you should have on your page.

You can think about usability, and trying to make sure that the design of the site is good. That's good for users, and for search engines. You can think about how to make your site faster. Not only does Google use site speed and rankings, as one of the many factors that we use in our search rankings. But if you can make your site run faster, that can also make it a much better experience. There are an enormous number of things that SEOs do. Everything from helping out with the initial site architecture, and deciding what your site should look like, the URL structure, the templates, and all that sort of stuff. Making sure that your site is crawlable. All the way down to helping optimize your return on investment.

Trying to figure out, what are the ways you're gonna get the best bang for the buck, doing AB testing. Trying to find out what is the copy that converts. There's nothing at all wrong with all of those methods. Now, are there some SEO's who go further than we would like, sure. And are there some SEO's who actually try to employ unfriendly techniques, sure.

Bad Practices:

People that hack sites, or keyword stuff to repeat things. Or they do sneaky things which redirect, are looked down upon. But our goal is to make sure that we return the best possible search results we can. And a very wonderful way that search engine optimizers can help is by cooperating and trying to help search engines find pages better. SEO is not spam. SEO can be enormously useful. SEO can also be abused and it can be overdone. But it's important to realise that, we believe in an ideal world, people wouldn't have to worry about these issues. But search engines are not as smart as people, we're working on it. We're trying to figure out what people need. We're trying to figure out synonyms, and vocabulary that people use so that you don't have to know exactly the right word to search for, to find exactly what you want. But until we get to that day, search engine optimization can be a valid way to help people find what they're looking for, via search engines.

You always have to take what Matt Cutts says with a grain of salt, right. He has to speak on behalf of Google. He has to talk to the masses. You have to take it within context a little bit. But for the most part, the part I'm trying to convey here is that, SEO is not this manipulative thing that Google doesn't like. It's very acknowledged and accepted in the community. There's a big spectrum right now between SEO experts. There's a group of people doing great things, and also people who are circumventing the rules, breaking the rules, breaking the law sometimes. Keep that in mind.

Percentage of People that click on Organic VS Paid Results

Every industry is different, and every SEO will probably tell you something different. There's been a lot of different studies, but in general there's about a 70/30 split, between paid and organic search. Typically, paid results receive 30% of the clicks, whereas organic results receive the majority, 70% of the clicks.

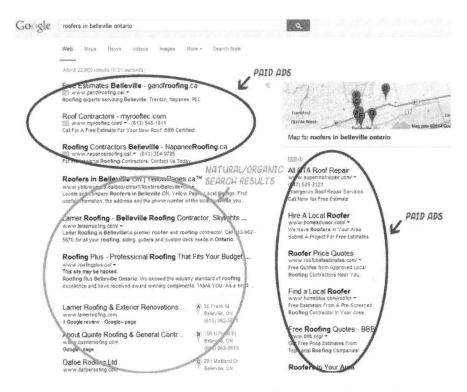

However, this really varies, depending on what industry you're in. Some people say this is totally off, some people say this is dead accurate. This is sort of the guide that most of the industry uses. Every year a new click through rate study comes out.

Organic – Click through Rates by Ranking

There was actually a data leak, at AOL. And people took all this data from the search engine, and they tried to put together a click through rate chart. Basically trying to determine, what is the number 1 ranking worth. What is the number 2 ranking worth? And ever since then, there have been a lot of studies. These are usually marketing agencies that conduct these studies, and there's a lot of variations.

When Google changes the search engine results page, google listing click through rate changes as well. Google displays different page layouts depending on that type of search. For eg, local search results come with up to 7 map listings as well. We call this the local pack, we find that these listings are highly correlated with your organic rankings. In general, about 35-40% of all clicks will go to the first result on the page - if all else is equal.

Rank #	Average CTR	Median CTR
1	36.4%	25.0%
2	12.5%	9.1%
3	9.5%	7.1%
4	7.9%	5.5%
5	6.1%	3.8%
6	4.1%	2.7%
7	3.8%	2.6%
8	3.5%	2.0%
9	3.0%	1.8%
10	2.2%	1.5%

Those CTR can be impacted by Google review ratings. But the big take a way here is that the top 3 results take ~60% of all the queries. And the top 5 take about 75%.

That shows us that Google typically delivers highly relevant results - that's why 75% of clicks, are going to the top 5 results. We're much more likely to change our search phrase, than we are to go to page 2, or page 3.

If you outsource your SEO to an agency, a lot of the times sneaky agencies will say. Yeah we have you on page 2 for 100 keywords. But in reality, because click through rates are so low, on the second page and even on the bottom 5 results, you're still invisible, if you're that low in the search.

People are really only sifting through the top 5 results, is what makes SEO so important today. You have to be in the top 5, or you're nowhere.

How a Website is displayed in Search Queries

Title tag ➡ Dentist in Richmond, BC | Lansdowne Dental & Implant ...
www.lansdownedentists.com/ ▾
Display URL Richmond's Best Dental and Implant Clinic. We specialize in dental implants, crowns, bridges, teeth whitening, and other family & cosmetic dentistry. ◥ Meta Description

So this is what we're gonna be talking about, when we use a lot of jargon today. When we talk about Title tags, this is the search snippet that we're talking about.

The Heading "Dentist in Richmond…" is the Title Tag, the display URL below that in green and below that is the search snippet, or the meta description, are some of the things we'll be covering today. We don't need to go through all of this, but there's a number of different algorithm updates that Google has created over the last decade or so.

As we said earlier, the search engine algorithm updates more than once a day, with minor updates that we probably don't notice. But roughly every year and a half to 2 years, are major algorithm shifts. Where they significantly change how they're doing things and it really throws people of.

The Mobile Update, Pigeon, Penguin, Hummingbird, Panda, florida update. Some of them are very controversial because, the Florida update was really tricky. Because they did it November, and it really threw off people's estimate for the holiday. There are a lot of e-commerce sites that got burned during Christmas, because Google changed their algorithm in November. All of a sudden everyone lost their search engine positions. We don't need to go through all of this. But the point is that, if you got really into SEO and you studied it for 5 years, and then you stopped. You stopped learning; you stopped staying up to date with it. You would be out of the loop, within a year, maybe even less. Because the algorithm is always changing, its emphasizing different things.

SEO is the kind of practice that you need to constantly, keep yourself updated with. Numerous algorithm updates over the last decade have occurred, because Google realized very early on that search would become the back bone of everything they do. Google does a lot now. There's Google maps, Google docs, Google Phones: Androids, and they're in a lot of different areas. There's Google drive that goes head to head with Dropbox, Google Glass.

I mean they do everything.

But search is the back bone of everything they do.

Big Picture View

What really matters?

If we had to take an elevator ride, and I had 60 seconds to explain SEO to you, this is what I would say. If you want to walk away from this presentation right now, and you only want to know one thing, this is what you need to know.

Explaining SEO in 60 seconds.

1. *The titles of your pages are important*

2. *The links pointing back to your website are important*

3. *The relevancy of your content matter*

4. *Your reputation and credibility matters*

5. *Social media matters*

6. *Freshness matters*

7. *The words used in those links are important*

8. *Your ability to get pages into search indices is important*

SEO is about 60% Art, 40% Science. With optimization, everyone has to play by the set of rules that Google has laid out. However, once you are past that, a lot of search engine optimization really comes down to creative you can be in your traffic acquisition.

It's no secret that there's been plenty of clashes between SEO agencies, and their clients. SEO agencies have kind of a bad reputation sometimes, and then the clients are very notorious for not understanding the process at all. The point is that, search engine optimization is not straight forward, and you can rarely guarantee a top ranking. Any good SEO will never guarantee a specific top ranking especially for a highly competitive position. You're at the whim of the algorithm, and things can change instantly.

Because of that, clients are often very demanding and they say, I want this. And the agencies often have to say, we can't give that to you, but we can try. And that happens very often

Here's an exaggerated yet example of the tension between the two parties:

> *SEO Company: Hello, Welcome to Top SEO services, how may I help you.*
> *Client: Number 1 on Google. I want to be number 1 on Google. I need to be number 1 on Google.*
>
> *SEO Company: I'm sure we can help, but first I need to find out, a little more about your website.*
> *Client: I just want to be number 1 on Google.*
> *SEO Company: Sure. I will need to ask you a few important questions. Can you tell me what key word you want to be number 1 for?*

Client: Credit Cards. I want to rank number 1 on Google, for credit cards. Can you do it?

SEO Company: That's a very competitive key word. Can you tell me a little more? What is your URL? Client: www. Simple-credit-cards-made-easy- for-you.info. Can you get me number 1?

SEO Company: Hmm..How old is your domain?
Client: One week old, and I want to be number 1 this week.

SEO Company: Yes. Perhaps we can look at some other key words for you first, and then work on the credit card key word later.

Client: No I'm not interested. I want to be number 1 on Google for credit cards. I want to be number 1 this week.
SEO Company: But we could get you more traffic in less time, if we target some longer tail keywords.

Client: I don't care.

SEO Company: If you let us do our keyword research, we can get you the number 1 page ranking on Google, for hundreds of higher converting key words, that will make you more money.

Client: I don't care.

SEO Company: We can make your website print money like clockwork if we target some longer, specific keywords with good traffic that are less competitive.

Client: I don't care about any of that.
SEO Company: Okay fine. Then why the hell do you want to be number 1 on Google, for credit cards anyway?

Client: So I can sell a $17 E-book. I'm an affiliate, and I want to get rich quick.

SEO Company: Are you kidding me?

Client: No.
SEO Company: Have you thought this through? No.

Client: No
SEO Company: You want to rank number 1 on Google, and compete with big banks, and institutions who are willing to spend millions of dollars, to sell a $17 e-book. And you will probably only make 50% commission.

Client: I want to be number 1 on Google.

CHAPTER 5
DIGGIN' INTO SEO: ON PAGE FACTORS

1 **On Page Optimization**

On Page Optimization, a.k.a the stuff on your page. So let's get into the meat of it. We're going to delve into:

1. *keyword research, and searcher intent*

2. *the title tags*

3. *meta description tags*

4. *heading tags*

5. *image optimization*

6. *body content*

7. *internal link anchor text.*

The really simple way to think about On Page Optimization is that it is everything that you have direct, 100% control of. Remember the break down the 60% Art, 40% Science breakdown?

This is the Science. This is where we all play by the same rules. The algorithms looking for the same thing, across all web page, right. Before we get started, I want to convey the most important point. Which took me probably 2 years to figure out. I definitely did this the wrong way. The problem when people first get into Search Engine Optimization, they get really excited with their new powers.

They feel giddy & excited, "I'm gonna get my site ranking number 1. This is great!" They completely overdo it. They do their keyword research and they say, okay I want to rank for rainbow cat. I'm gonna be number 1 for rainbow cat, and they buy rainbowcat.com/rainbowcat, and I'm gonna title my page, rainbowcat.

I'm going to make my header rainbow cat. And I'm gonna mention rainbow cat 20 times on the page. They completely overdo it. I've seen plenty of lawyers, dentist, cleaners etc. do the exact same thing by listing their keywords everywhere.

I get it, they are writing for search engines but it's very wrong. This is something that worked a while back, but search engines have now grown up and gotten smarter.

The much better way for search engines, is also better for your users, and it usually ranks you higher. The most important aspect of On Page Optimization is to write compelling copy first, and then optimize. You really want to be designing for users. You write content and you put it on the web. You want to be writing it for people that will actually read it. And you want to take these search engine optimization principles, and apply them afterwards. Don't go into it thinking, how can I get the search engine to rank this well. You want to go into it thinking, "how can I write something great. How can I write something awesome? That people will love to read, and consume and share, and all that". Then go back and tweak it. Tweak it so that it fits with what the search engine is looking for.

2. Keyword Research

Keyword Research is one of the most important parts of On Page Optimization. You start this from the Google AdWords Keyword Planner tool, which is sort of the default tool of the SEO industry

You access it by going to adwords.google.com and clicking on the tools section and then selecting the "Search for new keyword and ad group ideas" option under the Keyword Tool. This becomes one of the most used tools that I ever use in SEO. This will give you all of the volume data. It tells you the number of times, people are searching for a particular keyword. The most important piece that I want to point out is that this tool also gives you good key word ideas. Terms that people are entering into Google that you might have not been aware of.

The tool also distinguishes between Exact, Phrase & Broad match.

If I type in red shoes, and it says exact match a thousand times, then a thousand people have typed in red shoe. A phrase match means that query has been typed in with those words, in that order, but there can be words around it. Phrase matches are usually much bigger; if I type in red shoes, it will also show me results for cool red shoes, red shoes for sale. Broad match is anything that Google thinks, is related to red shoes. So red shoes, but it would also include red sneakers, red boots, maybe marooned sandals. If you use broad or Phrase match, your data gets really, really, inaccurate. 0 just keep that in mind when you do it.

When I do my keyword research, I like to start with a large list, of really broad keywords. I download as many as necessary, from the Google AdWords keyword tool, and I combine them into one file. I start deleting unnecessary keywords, and I really think about the searcher intent. And then I refine my list, plug it back into the keyword tool and repeat.

3. Understanding Searcher Intent

The most important aspect of this here is to really consider Searcher Intent. And I like to break searcher intent into 4 different categories.

1. *Navigational queries.*
2. *Information queries*
3. *Commercial Research queries*
4. *Ready to buy queries.*

A Navigational search is usually a query that, maybe someone has been to the website before, and they're just trying to get there again. They've been there a couple times, and they want to get there. Or they know of something, and they're just trying to navigate their way to it, right. A really good example of this is Facebook log in. Someone's typed in Facebook log in, they know what they're trying to get.

They've been at that page before. They're using the search engine to navigate to their query. Here's some quick examples.

Search Intent Examples:

1. Navigational Queries- "Vancouver Tourism office hours"
2. Information Queries- "Things to do in Vancouver"

3. Commercial Research queries- "Hotels in Vancouver"

4. Ready-to-buy Queries- "Book Travel Package Vancouver"

A **Navigational Query** might be Vancouver Tourism office hours. Maybe they've been to the Vancouver Tourism website before. They're just trying to get there again and look at the office hours again.

Information Queries they're usually not commercial in nature, and they're just people trying to do research - things to do in Vancouver. Now that being said, even though Information queries are generally non-commercial in nature. There are some companies that use this principle really well. A great example of this is Trip Advisor. You type things to do in any US city; Trip Advisor is usually in the top 3 and they give a great landing page experience.

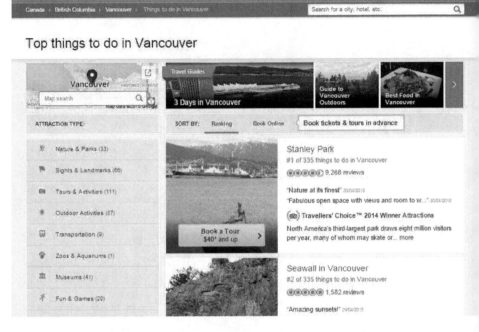

Eg: The top things to do in Vancouver – Stanley Park, Seawall, Granville Island, Queen Elizabeth Park.

They list all these things, and then on the front it's plastered with ads for Expedia, and different hotels you can book. The point here with Information query, people that do SEO really well, they create really great landing pages for Informational Queries.

They then answer the user's questions while, also trying to sell them. They provide a lot of really good content, and then they end it with, "By the way we are blah, blah, company, and we're selling blah, blah".

Commercial Research and **Ready-to-buy** queries are

examples of phrases that are very commercial in nature. The user, they have their credit card out, they're ready to go.

For Ready to buy query, they want to end their search, they want to make the purchase as soon as possible, therefore, they include "pay" or "buy" or "book appointment" within their search query. These are the keywords where you'll see a lot of Search Engine Marketing spend. You'll see a lot of pay per click ads on phrases like this, and a lot of people competing. It's very cut throat for a lot of these queries. The point here is that when you're doing Keyword research, the first thing small business owners should do is keyword research. You really do want to consider, what's going on in the head of the searcher.

With keyword research, find search terms with significant volume in your city and then pick the top search terms that bring in majority of the traffic. It's also not feasible for small business owners to be ranked for national or state/provincial terms immediately. Just because "car dealerships California" is being searched 20,000 times a month, it doesn't mean you can immediately rank number one for it. Start with your city, and then expand if it is feasible in your budget.

4. Title Tags

1. *Easily the most important aspect of on-page optimization.*
2. *Title Tags tell humans (and search engine spiders) what the page is about.*
3. *Should be approximately 50 characters long.*
4. *It's rumoured that the primary keyword should be as close to the front as possible (but always designed for users).*
5. *Titles should be unique for every page.*

This is, in terms of On Page Optimization, the most important aspect of On Page Optimization. Title Tags tells humans, and search engines spiders, what that page is about. It's rumored that the primary keyword should be, as close to the front of the page as possible. I'm not sure how true that is. But really you should just be designing for users. You need to be doing whatever makes the most sense for the user. Title should be unique for every page. Whenever I want to look at really good examples of On Page Optimization, or SEO in general, I love to look at Yelp. Yelp does a really good job of this. If you type coffee shop San Francisco, Yelp ranks really well for it.

This is the title tag. A lot of times we say okay, title tags and people say, oh the title tag. You mean the big title on the homepage right? - no.

We're talking about the browser title. "Best Coffee shop San Francisco, CA" on the browser. In terms of On Page Optimization, your title tag is probably the most important and needs to incorporate your primary search terms so that it shows as the header on the search results:

Best coffee shop San Francisco, CA - Yelp

www.yelp.ca/search?find_desc...**Coffee+Shop**...**San+Francisco%2C**... ▼
Reviews on Best coffee shop in San Francisco, CA Blue Bottle Coffee, Sightglass
Coffee, Graffeo Coffee Roasting Company, Philz Coffee, Four Barrel Coffee, ...

5. <u>Meta Descriptions</u>

1. *Should only be about 150 characters*
2. *Your primary keyword should be in the tag(because Google bolds keywords in the query)*
3. *Meta description DOES NOT impact rankings, but can significantly alter click-through rates*
4. *The meta description does not appear anywhere on the page*
5. *Google will often supplement content on the page, rather than the Meta description. If it either does not find the description tag, or finds the keyword on the page, and wants to display it to the user.*

The Meta Description tag is one of the few pieces of On Page Optimization that matters, but you don't see anywhere on the page. The page is in the code. It should be about 150 characters long. Your primary keyword should be in there, because if it is, then Google will use the tag and then bold it.

You've got to understand Meta descriptions do not influence rankings, for the most part. But they can significantly alter click through rates. This is the little search snippet that your users are seeing in the search engine. And this is going to be the thing that their eyes glance over.

They basically make a snap decision on which link to click, and this is what they're going to be looking at.

Title tag ➡️ Dentist in Richmond, BC | Lansdowne Dental & Implant ...
www.lansdownedentists.com/ ▾
Display ↗️ Richmond's Best Dental and Implant Clinic. We specialize in dental implants, crowns,
URL bridges, teeth whitening, and other family & cosmetic dentistry. ↖️ **Meta Description**

Now here's the warning.

Google will often supplement content from the page. If someone types something in and your page is relevant for that and it ranks well, but that keyword is not in your Meta description, Google will send a spider to your site, and find where that's mentioned on your site, and replace the Meta description with your content. This can throw some people off, because it's a really good practice to write a good Meta description. And a lot of people, put a lot of time and effort into writing, the perfectly crafted, click through rate driving Meta description. And sometimes Google won't use it.

6.   Heading Tag

1. *Heading Tags are used to logically lay out your web page.*

2. *Primary keyword should be included at least once in the heading tag.(does not need to be ab exact match)*

3. *Like all aspects of SEO, don't overdo it.*

4. *H1 tags seem to be less important today, but still worth optimizing*

5. *H2, H3, H4, H5, etc…tags also exist, but seem to have less influence on rankings.*

Heading tags are used to sort of logically lay out your web page. The primary keyword or a closely related keyword should be included at least once, if it makes logical sense. This is one of the things that's often very overdone.

A lot of people who over optimize their pages; they also use H2, H3, H4, H5. I'm not saying you shouldn't do that necessarily. But just don't overdo it, cause it gets over done so much. If you were trying to rank really well for coffee shop San Francisco, people who over-optimize would have "Coffee shop San Francisco", as their H1 tag and then a bunch of content. Then coffee shop San Francisco as their H2 tag with a bunch of content, and then coffee shop San Francisco, as their H3 tag and so on.

Don't do that. That's designing for search engines. We don't want do that. We want be designing for the user. This is what we're talking about, when we talk about the H1 tag. Coffee shop San Francisco mentioned once, and it's wrapped in an H1 tag.

7.   The Importance of Content

Stop worrying about optimizing throughout your content. Today, it's riskier than ever to overdo it. Please, do NOT stuff your keyword everywhere. Keep keywords within 2%.

Any more than that and you risk incurring some on-page penalty – and with these, it's tricky because you won't tank in the search results, you'll just be held back (so you won't even know it).

Include your main keyword once, preferably in the opening sentence/paragraph, and bold it. It's a good idea to bold more than once; underlining and italicizing is rookie, looks bad, and makes Google more suspicious.

Dominate your niche; always tie each post back to your core theme, even though not every post or page should be going after specific keywords; think buyers; what are they searching for? Create the ultimate resource and you can't *not* win long-term.

Incorporate the keywords that you determined in your Keywords Research that were worth chasing after. Remember, variety is the name of the game. You never want to overdo anything or become robotic. The following are some guidelines that were shared to me by one of my mentors, and a great copywriter:

- **Unique content only.** Friendly reminder, never plagiarize or swipe content OR USE A SPINNER. Modeling and rewording is fine, but every sentence has to be unique.

- **Write naturally.** This is for the end user, not Google. Do not keyword stuff or overdo it with phrases you want to rank for. Use lots of synonyms.

- **Let it flow.** Get something down. Then edit like a crazy person, as the days and weeks pass by. Eighty percent of effective copywriting is editing.

- **Find your voice.** Speak to your ideal customers' pain points—and write with a real personality that stands out—you'll find even more success.

- **Clear, consistent call to action.** Ideally, each page should have a phone number at the top and a quote form (or applicable opportunity to become an email lead, depending on niche)

- **Leverage sense-based descriptors.** You have 5 senses, believe it or not. Don't limit yourself by only thinking about how something looks. How does it feel? Sound? Taste? Smell?

- **Annihilate your verbs (boosts uniqueness).** This tip will take you from "me too" to "bomb diggity"... and social shares earned with silky smooth copy means more phone calls. And more phone calls, means more money.

- **Murder your metaphors (boosts uniqueness)..** An example: the sugar-free Red Bull to your shot and- a-half of Grey Goose, pairing the right local business with our Local Mogul Model results in serious synergy.

- **Avoid Clichés (boosts uniqueness)..** If you start typing and think, "hmm, everyone says that," go back and edit. Be UNCOMMON. Nobody gives a shit about bland. Think purple cow.

- **Use alliteration (boosts uniqueness)..** Daffy Duck, MightyMouse, Buffalo Bills, Circuit City, Profit Pimp—you feel my flow, Frank?

- **Place a safety net under your content.** Ask to call, fill form, get in touch!

8. <u>Body Copy</u>

This is all of the content on your page. Body copy is the meat of text on your website. Now there's really no minimum number of words needed. But in general, it's hard for search engines to make an assessment of your site, if there's not enough content right there on the website.

I recommend at least 150 words, could be more or could be a little less. You want to give the search engine an opportunity to rank your web page. Now I've seen a 50 word page outrank a 500 word page, it doesn't mean that more words is better.

Again, design for the users, but you do want to get as much content in there, as you can. As long as you're designing for users. Here's the big take away from this, and it's under the concept of keyword stuffing. The keyword you're targeting for, you really need to use it, 2 or 3 times. You don't need to go overboard. There's a million examples of people that did SEO in the past that did really bad job by stuffing keyword everywhere. The keywords would be used too many times. It would be mentioned awkwardly. Things that weren't good for the user. And usually the search engine catches up with you, that would not help you rank your small business.

However, this is sort of how archaic search engines used to work. They would say okay, in order to rank web pages, what's most relevant is the number of times something is mentioned. And that's why there were so many spammy results, back in the early 00's.

You'd see things like, buy shoes online, buy shoes online. And people would just mention it 100 times, and then that page would rank number 1 for buy shoes online. Just because it was more often, and that's really not how it works anymore.

Now you only need to mention it a couple times. Although we suggest keeping keyword density under 2%, there's no magic number, or text to code ratio. It just doesn't matter anymore – it's really about the user experience. You need to make sure your keyword is mentioned 2 or 3 times. Maybe 4-6 times if it's really long, but you don't need to worry about these obscure ratios.

Text to code ratio is another ratio, which looks at all he source code of your site and says, "Out of all the code, what percentage is text, and what is code?" Don't worry about these things; it's really not that big a deal.

Here's some thoughts from the Google Search Engine Oracle, Matt Cutts:

Matt Cutts: *Keyword density, let's talk about it a little bit. A lot of people think there's someone recipe, and you can just follow that like baking cookies. If you follow it to the letter, you'll rank number one, and that's just not the way it works.*

If you think that you can just say, okay I'm gonna have 14.5% keyword density, or 7%, or 77% and that will mean I'll rank number one. That's really not the case. That's not the way search engines rankings work. The way modern search engines, or at least Google is built is that the first time you mention a word, hey it's pretty interesting. It's about that word. The next time you mention that word it's like, "oh okay it's still about that word". And once you start to mention it a whole lot, it really doesn't help that much more. There's diminishing returns. It's just an incremental benefit, but it's really not that large. And what you'll find is, if you continue to repeat stuff over, and over again. Then you're in danger of getting into keyword stuffing, gibberish and those kind of things. The first one or two times you mention a word, then that might help with your ranking, absolutely. But just because you can say its 7 or 8 times, that doesn't mean that it will necessarily help your rankings.

The way to think about it is this. Think about the keyword that you'd like to have in your copy. Make sure your copy is long enough, that you can work those keywords into your copy in a natural way, and not an artificial way.

My recommendation is, to either read your content aloud, or read it to someone else. Or have someone else read it. And sort of say, do you spot anything that's artificial, or unnatural, or doesn't quite read right. And if you can read through the copy, and have it read naturally, where a person isn't going to be annoyed by it. Then you're doing relatively well. But you're going overboard if you're like one of these guys, where the copy is something like this: I know you're interested in red widgets, because red widgets are one of the best things in the world to have.

If you're an experienced SEO, you can really tell, whenever you land on a page that someone's just trying too hard to get the same phrase on the page, as many times as possible because it looks unnatural. Rather than helping, those types of practices will hurt your website. I would love it if people could stop obsessing, about keyword density. It will vary by area & by the type of industry.

There's not a hard and fast rule. And anybody who tells you that there is a hard and fast rule, you might be careful. Cause they might be selling you keyword density software, or something along those lines. I hope that helps. Maybe we can dispel that misconception, and people realize not to worry that much about it. Just make sure you have the words that you want to have on page. Make sure that they read naturally, and you should be in pretty good shape.

9. Internal Link Anchor Text

Internal linking is the last piece we'll cover for On Page Optimization. These are text links that link out to the different sections of your website. The text that you use to link matters. It's just one of the concepts that made Google different, from the other search engines.

Search engines factor in how you link to your content, as the clue to what that content is about. If you use text like "click here", "try this website", et cetera, you're not describing what that content is about. It's just too generic, you need to avoid that if you can and use descriptive link text - also known as Anchor Text, such as "family dentistry".

Internal links generally matter less than external links. Naturally if you're linking to your own content with a phrase, Google's going to value it a little bit less, than if another credible website does it.

Click depth is also important, so a page is more relevant, in a search engines eyes, if it's closer to the root domain.

www.mikecleaners.com/duct-cleaning is better than **www.mikecleaners.com/blog/home/duct-cleaning**

That doesn't mean you should go in and completely redo your website. But if you have a choice, **website.com/page.html** is considered more authoritative, than **website.com/folder/folder2/page.html**. That's just an apples to apples comparison. There's a lot of other factors, but if you have a choice, its best to get those pages to stay as close, to the root domain as possible. And a really good example of this is if you look at a lot of the SEO blogs, search engine land.com, one of my favorite geek sites. Almost all of their posts sit on the root domain. Any blog post that come out would be, search engine domain.com/name of post. Sometimes that's hard to do with the architecture, depends on your business goals. Depends on your company. Depends on a lot of other things, but it's just worth keeping in mind.

The location of the link is a strength factor as well. Google is getting really good at understanding site layouts. And they know the difference between a side bar link, and a footer link, a top navigation link, and a link that's in the content. All links are not created equal. You need to consider that. Links that are in the content of the page you're talking about is usually considered more valuable.

CHAPTER 6
DIGGIN' INTO SEO: OFF PAGE FACTORS

1. Introduction

Off Page Optimization is the other big piece of the equation. Search engines basically factor in how the rest of the internet views your website. In the past, this was simply described as link building, but it's become more comprehensive.

All things equal, the page with the most links wins. If all things were equal, there's 2 web pages that are exactly the same, and every single link is exactly the same. Then the page with more links is going to rank higher. However, there's a giant caveat. Relevant, quality links is the name of the game.

If all things are equal, all web pages were equal, and all links were the same. Then quantity would matter, but that's not the case. Powerful, authoritative, quality links is what it's all about.

If I have 2 web pages and they're pretty similar, and this one has 3 links. But the links are from a random tumblr page, your mom's Facebook page, and a silly blog comment. I only have 3 low quality links. This page is going to be out ranked by a page with a single link, from the CNN.com home page.

The quality and quantity of your links matters. Google's original algorithm mimics citation analysis. It was an examination of the frequency, patterns, graphs, of citations in articles and books. The way to think about this is that links are like citations, and lend credibility to the site they're pointing to. More good links mean higher ranking, and more traffic.

What Google basically did was to take the premise of citation analysis from university research papers, and apply it to the web. They said look, if links are like a citation, and the text of those links is the context of that citation, we can rank web pages based upon context & authoritativeness. That was the founding premise, as links are kind of like an academic citation.

The other concept is **Domain Authority**. The trust and authority of the domain, as well as the relevance of the content, are incredibly important. Links from relative, authoritative, trusted websites are generally quite valuable. Links from a generic Tumblr blog are not.

Google's getting real good at understanding how to value a link based upon its relevancy. They understand that if you are selling dental services, but you get a really high quality link, from an Audi dealership, then that doesn't make sense. Google will devalue that link because it isn't that relevant.

Back in the day, people would build link circles that would say "our partners" or something similar. The links would be between a dentist in Detroit, veterinarian in Tampa, shoe shiner in LA, and it just didn't make any sense. Of course that doesn't work anymore because Google is getting much better at understanding the contextual relevancy of these links, and it's worth thinking about when you're building links to your site.

2. <u>Simple Link Building Rules</u>

We're going to talk about a lot about different, link building strategies; keep these 4 concepts in mind:

<u>4 Simple Rules for Link Building</u>

1. *Get links from good, trusted, content*

2. *Don't get links from bad, spammy content*

3. *Link to good, trusted, content*

4. *Don't link to bad, spammy content*

That's the basic premise of this. You really want to think about your linking, and the way you build links. The way you think about neighborhoods. You really want to link to good neighborhoods and stay away from the bad ones.

3. Good Link Criteria

What's the criteria for a good link? Let's say we're selling San Francisco 49'ers jersey. We have our San Francisco 49'ers jersey website and we're trying to determine what a good link is so we can have strong some off-site optimization. Here's the questions I like to ask.

1. Is the link on a relevant site?

2. What's the overall topic of the domain?

3. What's the overall topic of the page?

4. What's the title of that page?

5. What's the content of that page?

6. What kind of sites are linked into that page?

Google is going to look at the pages that are linking to you, but they're also going to look at pages linking to that site. It goes further than you think.

You really want to think about this, from a neighborhood point of view. Is the link on a quality site? How old is the site? How many quality authoritative links, does that site have? Does Google trust it? A really good way to do a good sniff test for determining if the link is valuable is to see if it is ranking for its own keywords!

As we know, from earlier, the title tag is the most important aspect of on-page optimization. A really easy way to check if Google trusts a website is to go to that website, look at their title tag, see if there's a keyword in the title tag that they're optimizing for. Then Google it! Is that site ranking for their own keywords? If it is, it's usually indicative of the fact that Google trusts it.

It's a really easy way to determine whether Google trusts this website, and whether it is in a good neighborhood.

Check if it's ranking for its own keywords. Does the link have the keywords in the anchor text? Are you getting a link that says San Francisco 49'ers jersey? Or are you getting a link that says, "click here". Is the link pointing to the topical page? The internet is inherently very top heavy, which means that a lot of web pages have too many links, pointing to their home page. Not enough pointing to the deeper pages. Don't forget about your deeper pages. You really do want to link to your deeper content, if you can.

It's also important that links are long lasting and don't churn. Great links that disappear will drop rankings. If you build up a lot of links, and then they start to disappear over time. If they're lower quality, or they're blog comments, that the webmaster is removing then having a lot of churn in your links is no good. You want to accrue a steady number of links over time, in a natural way. You don't want to gain 50, and then 5000, and then 0, and then lose a bunch, and then gain a bunch. You want a steady acquisition of links as Google tracks this – known as link velocity in the SEO world.

4. <u>Synthetic vs. Natural Link Profiles</u>

At the end of the day, link profile should be natural. One of the best quote I ever heard about link building was, "all *link building is grey hat*". White hat search engine optimization is when you play by all the rules, and you do everything by the books. Black hat search engine optimization is, when you break the rules and you do sneaky stuff. Grey hat is somewhere in between. And a lot of people say that, all link building is grey hat. When you're building links to your site, and you're using good anchor text, that sometimes can get into grey area stuff, but that's okay. The point is that you don't want to overdo it.

An example of bad link building, is if you get 50 new links in one day. That all say San Francisco 49'ers jersey, that's not natural. That's very synthetic. It's going to send a trigger to the search engine. So it's just too much, too soon.

However, if you get 2 links per day, over the course of 2 months, with very natural sounding phrases, like *great 49'ers jerseys, NFL jerseys for 49'ers fans, cool jerseys, San Francisco 49'ers jersey for cheap*. That's good.

I'm a huge fan of what's called *Partial Match*, and *Branded Partial Match Anchor Text.*

Partial Match examples. If my keyword is knee replacement cost, and my company name is Formosa Medical Travel. I would optimize for keywords like cost of knee replacement, total knee replacement price, comparison prices knee replacement surgery, TKR, acronym for total knee replacement, TKR price, TKR cost.

Branded Partial Match is when you incorporate the company name as well. So Zappos for example, rather than link into their site, with *buy shoes online* over, and over again. *Shoes for sale Zappos, Zappos discounted shoes*. All these different variations are what I like to call Partial Match. So you get a piece of the keyword in there, and incorporating your brand name is good as well. Google cares about branding.

5. <u>No-Follow vs. Do-Follow Links</u>

Blogs became really popular, really easy to set up, really accessible for a lot of different people, and then spam came. It was pretty typical 5, 10 years ago for a lot of spam to be on blog comments and things like that. And so Google came out with a new tag. They basically created what's called the *"rel=no follow"* tag. So they created a new tag to still let people link, but without letting any of the authority of the website pass through to the next site.

We previously discussed the idea of how Google attributes a value on a link. Effectively what it does is, you append it to a link, and it doesn't pass the value of that site. Everything still looks the same, the links are still there, and people can make their contribution. However, you don't get the juice, the authority, from the link to your website.

A lot of out of the box Content Management Systems come with this setting on default. For example, when you set up a WordPress blog, it will default to this. It will add a no follow tag. When you place a link on someone's WordPress blog, it will not pass link authority onto your website.

So a lot of websites default to this now. What this did was, this created a culture of what people call *"do follow links"*. And that's what's funny about search engine optimization. Google does something to try and prevent manipulation, and all these other things. Usually creates this like round about culture, where people just try and get around it. So what happen was, Google created this *"no follow"* tag, and then people basically say okay. Then I only want links that don't have the no follow tag. We've nicknamed them "do follow" links. That created people, who only went for do follow links. But here's the problem. Search engines really expect healthy mix, of "no follow" and "do follow" links. Actual ratios are debated, and what they're looking for is debated. The rule of thumb is, your link profile should look natural. If you have 100 links, and all 100 of them are not "not follow", or "do follow" it just looks fake. It looks synthetic.

It looks like you're buying links, or you're doing something manipulative. You have to keep that in mind. Here's the other part that gets confusing. Google claims that no link juice uses past through. However, it's fairly well documented, that there are instances where it does pass through. There's a couple of cases that is out there, about people creating websites, and they get a single link from Wikipedia - all Wikipedia links are no follow links; There are cases, where people would get one link from Wikipedia, and their ranking would sky rocket.

Whenever you listen to what Matt Cutts says, you have to take it with a grain of salt because he has to represent Google's best interests. They can't say, "Oh! We're doing this now, or we're not doing this now." They do need to be a little bit secretive. Otherwise people would just reverse engineer everything that they do. They claim that the no follow tags don't pass page authority, but in some instance, they do.

Yes, this can get confusing but here's the rule of thumb: Build links like its 1996- when we really didn't rely on search engines as much. We really went into our industry specific verticals and forums, and where we found people that are like minded to us, with them we exchanged links, and sent people to the right resources.

That's the strategy you wanna take. Build links like its 1996, when we didn't rely as heavily on search engines. Sometimes the best traffic is referred traffic, from your backlink building. So focus on getting links for traffic and you won't have to worry about this at all. You don't need to factor in all these things we talked about, when you do your link building. The point is, if you get a link that's bringing meaningful traffic, and people are converting on your website. Do you even care if it's no follow or do follow? It really doesn't matter at that point. So it's good to understand these principles. My point is that you internalize this principle with your link building efforts.

6. Recovering From Bad Links

How to Recover from Bad Links

1. *Give it time.*

2. *Request to have them taken down & use Google Disavow feature*

3. *Take down the page (if it's not the homepage)*

4. *Consistently build more good links.*

5. *Setup a 301 redirect and get a new domain.*

How to recover from Bad Links? Sometimes people get really ambitious, they outsource some of their link building, and acquire a lot of really bad links. They don't understand SEO and they build links, and then they learn more about it and realize the plethora of crappy links that they've already bought that hurt more than they actually help their rankings.

There's a couple of ways to recover from them. First you just give it time. The value of a link seems to decrease over time, so just waiting it out can be helpful. You can request to have them taken down. Often times you or someone that you hired in the past built links on really spammy websites, sometimes you can contact the webmaster and say ask that you noticed you're linking to Viagra links and would liked to be removed. Of course majority of the time you'll have 100s if not 1000s of these type of links. In that case you may have to take down that page that is linking to all these hurtful links. Some people call this SEO amputation. Where if you have a page, of course you can't do it with your root domain, but if you have website.com/keyword.html and you have all these bad links pointing to that page. Just delete the page, or amputate it. That's one way.

Google now has a "Disavow tool" where you send them a list of all spammy links that you think are hurting your website. Google then devalues this tool if their algorithm hasn't picked up on it already.

Consistently building more good links. So if you have 20 good links and 5 bad links one month, and then the next month you have 50 good links, and 5 bad links. Your good link ratio is better, that's good.

In the worst case scenario, if all of your efforts haven't been able to do anything to improve your rankings, setting up a 301 redirect and pointing it to a new domain works would do the trick.

7. Creating A Resource (The Wikipedia Way)

Why does Wikipedia usually rank at the top, the first result, or the top 3? There's 2 schools of thought on it. One, as people just make the claim that Google has a bias towards Wikipedia. That they just have manipulated the results, and sometimes they just allow Wikipedia to rank. I don't know if I believe that, some people say that. If Google was doing that, I would be okay with that because Wikipedia is just such a fantastic source, but I don't think Google is doing that.

Wikipedia is honestly ranking well on its own, in a lot of different scenarios and here's why:

You think about the origins of Google, and how they got started. The real premise behind it was they sort of looked at links as a very important, piece of the puzzle. You think about links as citations, if you think about it in an academic way. The more frequently something is cited in academia. They took this principle and said, if a lot of other resources are citing it, it's probably a good resource. It's under that principle that you should think about search engine results as well. Backlinks are the online version of citations.

Wikipedia is very, very, frequently linked to. What it comes down to is Google has created their business model around consistently, and reliably answering the user's question. Therefore, when people type in search queries, they find what they're looking for on Google, and they repeat that process over & over again, that gets reinforced. Google's core business basically monetizes around search engines. It is in their best interests to deliver the most relevant information time and time again.

Wikipedia is always answering people's question. It's amazing resource, people contribute to it for free, and it's not always necessarily right.   I mean it's a lot of contribution. It gives a lot of the facts, and then it cites other resources. In terms of Google's point of view, Wikipedia is the perfect example, of answering the user's question. The fact that it's a really good resource, combined with the fact that it's frequently linked to and has tonnes of relevant content.

Often times there aren't a lot of websites that should out rank Wikipedia. It is the most relevant thing. It is the most relevant starting point, for someone who's doing a search. To summarize, people think Google is manipulating the rankings, and biasing it towards Wikipedia. That may not be true.

What is true is that Wikipedia is often answering the user's question, therefore, it should deserve to be number one very often. I really like, and I've had experience in the past, of when I create a really good resource for users. It ranks really well.   A lot of people think about website optimization the wrong way. They don't want to link out to their competition. They don't want to link out to other site. They want to drive links to their site, but they don't want to link out. However, whenever I create a really good resource for the user, I link to relevant content. I link to stuff, that's helpful to the user. I always find myself ranking higher.

Now does this mean, if you create a website and you link to Wikipedia, you're gonna rank number one, instantly. No, not at all. It's not that straight forward. However, if you are linking to really good resources for users, Wikipedia being one of many. I find that when the search engine spiders seem to come to the site, they see all of the links and they sort of put the site in a really good link neighbourhood. I like to do that, especially with a new site. Cause I like to build a lot of links, to really relevant, trusted, authoritative, resources on the web. Give my website, that association with good content. That's one of the strategies I like to use so I would recommend doing that.

8. <u>Link Building Tactics</u>

There's an entire industry within SEO, which is the Link Building industry. There's a lot of different ways to do it. The way you go about link building, this is the art rather than a science, and there's a million different things you can do.

One of my favorite ways to get started is with **Guest blogging**. There are sites even dedicated to connecting people to guest bloggers. The premise is, people who own blogs constantly need new content. It's hard to come about lots of good content all the time. If you can create good content, and sort of weave in, or seed in your own anchor text, then you can create links for yourself.

For a dental clinic website, and I would want to get links pointing to my site for dental services in Toronto. I go to another dental website and say, "Hey, here's an article called the 7 ways to keep your gums healthy". I write the article, and then I end it with, Dr.Tony Smiles is a dental clinic in Toronto, and give myself a link.

That's the premise of guest blogging. There's 2 different ways to go about it though. One is called Horizontal guest blogging; the other is Vertical guest blogging. Vertical guest blogging is exactly what I just described. It's finding people in your industry, creating content for them, and placing a link back to yourself.

If run an auto parts store, for Horizontal Guest blogging, I would find a blog on antique cars. I write a great article, on how rotating the tires of antique cars every 6 months helps them last longer. At the end of the article, I end the article with a link back to the page on my site about classic car auto parts. That's your standard guest blogging opportunity. The problem is, people are usually in really small niches, and so they run out of websites to approach eventually. They run out of opportunities to get a link. A really clever way to go about this is called Horizontal guest blogging. Finding topics that aren't about what you do, but finding a way to relate, and link back to yourself. For example, I'm an organic food store owner. I just imported some awesome new broccoli from Eastern Europe. I'm trying to rank for the phrase, *Organic broccoli San Francisco.*

I've already reached out, and created articles for all the food bloggers in SF. They're getting annoyed, so I don't know where else to post. I have exhausted all of my vertical, guest blogging opportunities. How do I do Horizontal? Here's how I could do it. Now you're thinking, okay, I'm trying to rank for organic broccoli San Francisco. How could I get an article on a New Mom blog? How could I get an article on a video game blog, a music blog? Keep in mind that Broccoli helps you lose weight, increase focus, gets stronger and helps creative thinking.

Here's how you can link broccoli with seemingly unrelated niches:

A New Mom blog- an article on losing baby weight, and including broccoli as one of the 7 options that you list.

Video game blog- Write an article on 5 foods that heighten awareness, while playing video games, and include a link to organic broccoli.

Music blogs- Create a post on inspiring creativity. Include long walks on the beach, smoking what musicians smoke, and eating this broccoli for heightened enlightenment.

Weight lifting blogs- A list of 10 foods that help lose weight, while working out, include the broccoli.

You can look at a blog, and be like, we're totally unrelated but figure out a way to sort of weave your content in there naturally. There's a lot of people that swear by guest blogging.

Blog Commenting

So this is pretty straight forward.

a) Find relevant blogs, contribute to the conversation, place a link.

b) Don't worry as much about no-follow/do-follow, just contribute to relevant topics, and mention your site, in a way that helps the reader.

Testimonials

When I first saw this idea, I loved it. Such a good idea. It's really straight forward. Think about all the products you've used in the last couple months. Go to those websites; find contact people and say, "Your products amazing, here's a quote from me. If you give me a link, you can publish it." You'd be amazed of how many people would take you up on that. If you're a dentist, reach out to dental equipment manufactures or a dental software you used. You don't have to lie about it. Do products you actually like - it's a great way to get links!

Getting Interviewed

If you are reading this book, you're a business owner or manager & are already an expert about something. There's a lot of local bloggers, news people that would love to interview you. A lot of the times, online publications will link to you. There's a site HelpAReporter.com. It's just a directory of people, that are willing to be interviewed by reporters. So it's a good way to build links if you're interested.

Content Marketing

This is a really good way to build links.

 a. Writing a "how- to"

 b. Create a "complete" guide or resource

 c. Create a top 10, top 100, top anything else

d. Debunk a myth "Biggest Misconceptions People have about a Dental Visit"

e. Link-out!

Writing a lot of these content pieces - lists, how to guides, and giving them to people, in order to get links is really good. People love lists. Human brains love when something is neatly organized, I always click on lists when I see them on Twitter, on RSS feeds. Debunking a myth is another good piece of content.

These are all under the premise, that you create it and give it out. But you can also create it, keep it on your site, and a lot of people will link to it. People just seem to love to link to these kind of things. I really love creating a really, good resource for people. Creating a page with a lot of links, a lot of information. People seem to always want to link to it.

The big secret about all of this, especially when you create comprehensive guides is that a lot of the times you don't have to write anything. You just have to collect it. You have to go around the internet, and find these awesome resources, and collect it for other people. It's a fantastic way to get awesome content - I recommend it.

Creating a Widget

This is a high risk (in terms of time), high reward strategy. Create a widget. I actually haven't done this myself, full disclosure. But I have some friends that have had unbelievable success with it. You basically create a widget that includes your link. If people really love it, it will spread around. Those links will sort of cascade through the web, if you can get it to hook. It's hard to get a lot of people to adopt your widget, but it can be beneficial.

Sponsoring a college club/ alumni newsletter

In the SEO world, people talk about all these strategies, for how they can coax college kids to give them links. People say all the time, yeah I sponsored this volleyball club at the State University by buying them pizza and beer and in return they gave me backlinks, it was awesome.

I met some guys at a conference, they did this. They found alumni newsletters in Universities, that also include the newsletter in an online version, and so they would sponsor it. They would get links back from the college – definitely a really clever way to get links.

Answer people's questions in forums/Q&A sites

These generally aren't great for rankings, but they can drive a lot of traffic. I don't really like Yahoo answers, Quora & Reddit can be great alternatives. Here, people may be asking questions that are relevant to the solution that you offer & you can provide them the guidance there.

Asking current customers

Asking current customers or your friends, or offline connections you've made. I really like working with offline connections. No one really trusts a random email, but people will trust you after you talk to them for 5 minutes. That's just kind a how we human operate – and it's definitely worth doing.

Linking Out

I said this twice, but it's proven to me over, and over again. The big mistake people make when they get into SEO is, they start to grasp how the ranking algorithms work, and then they say. Okay I'm not gonna link to anyone. I just want to acquire links, and acquire links, and acquire links and I'm not gonna link to anyone. I've always found that, the more I link to other people in my industry, including my competitors, my rankings always go up.

One of the first things I do when I start a new website, is link to a bunch of my competitors – as long as I'm being useful to the user. When you're creating your site, also link to your social media profiles or Web 2.0s, this includes Facebook, Twitter, Youtube etc.

Putting Tactics into Action

There are a few search queries that you can use to locate guest posting opportunities. One of the most common one is: "inurl:guest-post + keyword". This one is pretty straightforward. It is helpful for finding sites that allow guest posts on conversations about your keyword. The downside of this query is that you will sometimes end up with a list of guest posts that are related to your topic but it might be difficult for you to get your content published.

To combat that, you can focus you search on finding sites that are actively looking for guest posts. These sites tend to respond faster to emails enquiring about guest posting and are usually more willing to accept guest posts. Here are a few example queries:

Keyword + intitle:"write for us"
Keyword + intitle:"contribute to"
Keyword + intitle:"submit" + inurl:blog

CHAPTER 7
DIGGIN' INTO SEO: TECHNICAL OPTIMIZATION

1. Technical Optimization

Technical Optimization is all the stuff behind the scenes; your users don't usually see any of this. With the exception of URLs.

1. *Keyword-friendly URLs*

2. *The age of your domain*

3. *No duplicate content*

4. *www vs. non -www*

5. *Site speed*

6. *Freshness*

7. *XML Sitemaps*

SEO friendly URLs.

Let's say we're starting a fan site for Lady Gaga and we want to rank for the query Lady Gaga pictures. Well named web pages are good for users and search engines. So if you had a choice between these 3, which one you think would be the best?

It shouldn't be that difficult:

MyWebsite.com/content/folder2/page2054xr.html?cmd=home

MyWebsite.com/pics.html

GagaFans.com/lady-gaga-pictures/

Of course GagaFans.com/lady-gaga-pictures/. The first example of the URL structure are what many sites still use – these are basically the leftovers of the late 90's type of internet. It was so bad, it's much better now.

Years ago, keyword in the domain was a bigger ranking factor than it is now. However when you do a local google search you will find a majority of "exact match" or "partial match" domains ranking on the first page. Google made an algorithm update to matter less – however, there's still a little bit of a factor, but it's not as much.

When publishing a post on WordPress, adjust the permalink so it's less than 4 words, all lowercase, with a " - " in between each word (slight variations of your main keyword so it's not over-optimized).

If the permalink has already been published and the page or post is in Google's index, do NOT worry about changing it. Leave as is and make sure all new pages are done correctly.

2. Domain Age

The age of a domain, and whether or not that's a SEO factor, it comes up a lot. Personally I think it's a little bit over rated. I wouldn't worry about it that much. I think the age of your content, and the age of your links is more important.

A lot of people get in SEO, they look at their competitors and they say, "Oh my God, my competitor's domain is 7 years old. My domain is one month old". How am I ever gonna out rank them? It doesn't really work that way. Apples to apples, yes they do have an advantage over you. Although it is a small one in my opinion, you can do a lot of other things to get around that. The other factor that some people exists is that Google looks at your registration. When you register your domain name, it gives you options. 1 year, 2 years, 5 years, 10 years. People say, you should register for a long time, because that's indicating to the search engines, that you plan to stay around longer. I don't worry about these factors that much. I just wanted to point it out, because a lot of people will say, my website is new so I can't rank. I know that's not true. I had a client in a very competitive law niches are their brand new domain was ranked #1 on Google after just 6 months, when all their competitor's sites were at least 5 years old. Just worth keeping that in mind.

3. Duplicate Content

When one piece of content or one page of content is shown on multiple URL's. We call it Duplicate Content. Search engines have to decide which page to show, and they pick one winner. That's the big take away. You've got to think about this, from a search engines point of view. They want to deliver relevant results to the user. If I type something in, and I see the same article on 10 different webpages. That's a really bad user experience. It's in the search engines best interest, to pick one winner. So the point here is that, if you have a lot of duplicate content. You can sometimes reduce this penalty. A lot of small business owners think it's perfectly okay to take content from competitors and rehash to make it their own. That's will get you a slap from the Google Algorithm.

I was at a search engine conference a few months ago, and one of the speaker asked. Everyone in the room that works with a big company, raise your hand if you have duplicate content issues. 98% of the people raised their hands. It's a problem for everyone. A lot of websites actually generate duplicate content. There's a lot of problems that come about it. You want avoid it, whenever you can.

4. <u>Site Speed</u>

Site speed is proven to be a ranking factor. It's acknowledged now. First Google said that a fast site will help you rank higher. Nowadays, a better way to think about it is that a slow site will bring you down. Google has a site speed tool, you can go in and kind of check, all the boxes there. It's in Google webmaster tools, and that should help you out.

XML Sitemaps

XML site maps and XML files are submitted in Google webmaster tools to identify which areas of our site, you'd like them to crawl. You can also get a free one at xml-sitemaps.com. This help Google find any additional pages or content, they can't find on a crawl. Again, you do this in the Google webmaster tools.

Competitor Analysis

There are backlink tools that find links from your competitors. My 3 favorites are:

1. majestic.com

2. moz.com

3. ahrefs.com

These are sites where you can go in, type any domain name you want, and they'll show you all of their links. It's exactly where you want to start, when you're ready for off page optimization. Easiest thing to do is, type your competitors in these sites, and take their links. You want to take all of your competitor's links to get started.

Use the site colon option to find competitor title tags. Remember, title tags are one of the most important factors of On Page Optimization. If you type site: domain.com. What do you think a dentist in Seattle is optimizing their homepage for? This is an easy way to scan for your competitor's title tags. Checking their html site map. Every site doing SEO has a site map, in the bottom. You click site map. If they're doing good internal linking. Looking at the sitemap is an easy way to find competitor keywords.

Next is entering the URL into the Google keyword planner. If you go to the Google keyword planner and type the URL in - it will go to your site. It will crawl it, and it will say, "Hey! these are the keywords we think this page is about". Do this on your site to make sure that it knows you're optimizing for the right pages, as well as on your competitor.

Social Media SEO

The graph below was released by search metrics in 2014, showing the correlation of social media factors, for sites that were ranking in the top 30, for a number of different industries.

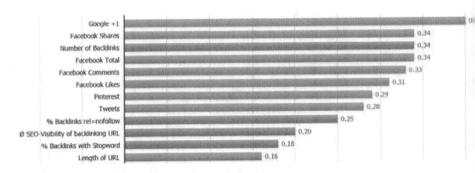

When these charts first came out people were surprised to see that social media signals have a big impact on rankings. Then Matt Cutts came saying that they don't look at Facebook data at a search engine conference. Someone right after came up on stage and said, yes you are and here's the proof and went on this long tirade, with all this research he had.

It's hard to say definitively, how much it matters but think about when Google first started.

They were looking for authority matrix in links. As a search engine, if someone is constantly sharing, liking, tweeting, retweeting, plus wanting a piece of content. If a piece of content is being shared, and retweeted and liked, in all these other different venues. Wouldn't you as a search engine want to know that?

To me, social media signals are indicators, of good quality content. Whether or not, they have a direct push and pull relationship on rankings I'm not sure. However, the general consensus seems to be, that the more social media engagement you drive into any page, the more rankings go up- up to a point of course.

There's some self-fulfilling prophecy in there too. Great stuff that's gonna rank as is, is likely to be shared a lot anyway. I kind of let the SEO nerds fight this one out, and remain on the safe side by publishing quality, helpful content for your customers. For now, just try and drive as many social media signals, to your pages as possible. It seems to help.

CHAPTER 8
LOCAL BUSINESS: REPUTATION & VISIBILITY

Reputation Management

How important is your business' reputation to you? Owning all of the shelf pace for your brand on Google is so important. A lot of small business owners have this problem. When we Google a business' name, we would see poor Google+ ratings, reviews that say XYZ Dealership sucks, hate XYZ Dealership, and competitors are ranking for your name, on the top 10. Whether or not that's rightfully so, should be debated elsewhere.

Reputation Management is owning the shelf space for your brand. Basically trying to get all 10 links for your name, or your query, or anything like that. There's a lot of different ways to do it. These are some really easy third party profiles. You can just set up, fill them out, and make them public. If your company name is a made up word, SEO for your brand name is super simple. You can rank for all 10 phrases within a couple days. There's a ton of different ways to do this. You can set up a blogspot, facebook page, Twitter, Tumblr etc. That way, google sees that your Brand Name is really trusted, as it has all these different social profiles, so it tends to rank really high.

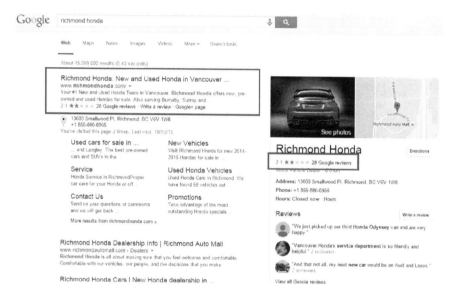

Regarding reviews on Google+, you can take steps facilitate more positive reviews. Prospective clients are using reviews more often than ever to determine if they should call the small business, monitoring your reputation has become paramount. The following are some sample approaches that can be taken to ensure 10+ positive Google+ reviews for all of your dental clinics:

• Follow-up calls made by company representatives inquiring about their experience

• Transcribe their response to facilitate posting of positive service reviews on Google+ by sending them an email with their review and Google+ review link of your page.

• Contact customers and then give them the opportunity to publish those reviews on multiple social media channels.

Some Interesting Facts for Online Reviews:

- **Trust**: 72% of consumers trust online review as much as word of mouth. (Local Consumer Review Survey)

- **The Bottom Line**: A difference of one "star" in the average rating in a typical online business profile can lead to a 5–9% difference in revenues. (Harvard Business Review)

- **Local Visibility**: 88% of consumers who search for local services on their mobile devices will call or visit one of the businesses they find within the next 24 hours.

One amazing statistic from this study, however, was the overall scrutiny now being put on the reputation of health practices and dentists. A whopping 32% (almost 1/3) of people had said they read reviews for dentists and doctors in the last year. But get this, 35% of consumers polled said they had used Google to search for a doctor in the last year, and 53% said that a practice's online reputation "mattered most" when selecting a doctor, which is even higher than the 51% that said the same thing about restaurants.

Local SEO

1. *Get your address on your site via contact page or footer*

2. *Register with Google places.*

3. *Sign up for Yahoo Local*

4. *Create an account at Bing Local*

5. *Reserve your Yelp page*

6. *Make a listing of Yellow pages*

7. *Register with City Search*

8. *Comment on local blogs*

9. *Guest blogs on local blogs*

10. *Give testimonials to local businesses*

This section is specifically for small business owners that have brick and mortar locations within a local city. What you basically want to do is, give the search engine an imprint of who you are, and where you are. Get your address on your site. Can be in your contact page or your footer – ensure that the listed NAP (Name, Address, Phone number) is exactly the same as one the Google+

.

pages and all other citations.

Make sure to register with Google places, Yahoo local, Bing local. Get your Yelp page, Yellow pages listing. Register with City Search. Then contribute on blogs that are local. Comment on local blogs. Do guest blogging, on local blogs. Give testimonies to local business websites. You want to convince the search engine that, this is where you are in this city.

Mobile SEO

This was a cool announcement that was implemented in April 2015. Mobile friendly pages will be given higher ranking in both mobile as well as desktop search. Google is desensitizing non-mobile formatted pages in mobile search, which makes complete sense. There is no surprise that Google expects mobile searching to surpass desktop searching any time now.

There's 3 ways to optimize your website for mobile devices.

1. Responsive design

2. Dynamic serving

3. Mobile URLs (with good canonicalization)

Responsive design is hot. Everyone talks about it. That's when you code your website initially, to fit any browser size. You can be viewing the website from 100s of different devices, and the websites will always look great. It's typically more expensive based on that feature. There's a lot of really good Responsive designs in WordPress themes out there.

Dynamic serving is when you do a user agent detection, to determine where to send the user. A lot of times, it is done in the header. It detects if you're on a mobile device, it sends you to X. If you're on a desktop, it sends you to Y.

The other version is having a **mobile URL**, so have an m.page. Where you basically say, okay website.com/page, or m.website.com/page, and canonicalize the mobile one, to the desktop one. You can look into this more. I just want to point out that, if you're in any space that's involved in mobile. Mobile search volume is taking off. Everyone's search is on mobile device, are going through the roof right now. There's a lot of different ways, where just on your design. Just catering to mobile, you can get a rank increase.

Useful SEO Tools

There's a number of products and services that my team & I personally use, whenever I'm starting an SEO campaign. I wanted to take you through them, and give you some guidance, on some of the tools you can use as well. The first is *Google Analytics.* This is a universal resource for discovering online insights. Small business owners, to all the way to large companies use this. Free enterprise grade analytics, highly recommend installing it on your website once it's online.

An additional analytics package that I really like is *Statcounter.* Statcounter is a good way to get a good snapshot of your traffic, on a day to day basis. Whereas Analytics is good for trends, and longer time period stuff, than looking at traffic over a long term.

Google Webmaster tools - This is how you'll effectively communicate to Google. It gives you a lot of different options, for submitting XML Site maps, and getting messages when you get penalties, your crawl rating index, and things like that. You definitely want to install Google webmaster tools.

Google keyword planner - This is where you'll start your keyword research training, new campaign. You input your keywords here and find the keywords that you'll be optimizing for. *Google Trends* is another really good way, to check macro, search volume trends, and search volume data whereas the Google keyword planner is more granular. I usually use Google Trends as a secondary tool, after the Google keyword planner.

If you do use WordPress, there's a lot of different really great themes out there. That's one of the reasons why I like it so much. I highly recommend checking *Themeforest.net, for* great looking WordPress themes.

For tracking your rankings, there's a lot of different software out there. A lot of people don't like to pay to track their rankings for multiple search terms, so a really good free option is, *Traffic Travis*.

If you're ready to do something a little more robust, and are willing to pay for a tool to track dozens of your search terms and potentially multiple websites, I like *Pro Rank Tracker*. This is a tool I use.

There's a lot of link analysis, and competitive link analysis tools out there. One of my favourite is *Majestic SEO.* It's a great tool for finding the links that your competitor have acquired. A great free tool, is *Open Site Explorer* to find your competitor's links – although for the free version, a good portion of the data might be outdated, it will still give very good insights. *Ahrefs* is another great one; this one's paid, but a very good tool for link analysis.

www.brokenlinkcheck.com is a free tool and it very quickly spiders your site, and searches for broken links. Especially after you've done a site migration, or moved a lot of stuff around. It's really good to use *it* and run it once on your site, it will show you any broken links that you might have.

Yoast or All in One Plugin is a fantastic WordPress plug in. I highly recommend installing this, it takes care of a lot of the work for you, if you're on a WordPress blog.

There's a lot of email retention, and email subscription tools out there. I personally like ***A Weber*** a lot for smaller businesses. If a large portion of your business comes from online channels then I would recommend ***Infusionsoft*** - it's the one I'm currently using. If you intend on building a large email list, I recommend these guys. You've probably seen it around a lot.

If instead of hiring someone, you'd like to stay up to date with SEO yourself, ***Search Engine Land*** is a great place to start. They have an insane amount out content as they send out a daily post that summarizes every major SEO story of the day. I recommend signing up for that. Another great SEO blog is ***MOZ.*** There's a lot of phenomenal tools that they have, and good blog post. It's certainly worth staying up to date, with what they're doing. Finally, I really also like ***www.lions.marketing*** *which is our website*. We do a phenomenal job of putting together SEO case studies, and emailing them out to people on our list. I highly recommend subscribing on our website.

This chapter basically concludes some of the SEO tools

that we use the most frequently and enjoy using for our clients.

CHAPTER 9
ADAPT YOUR BUSINESS & THRIVE

Adapt your business to the latest digital marketing business and unleash the full potential of your business growth!

You're still reading the book? But it's finished, and now you know more about search engine best practices and online small business marketing techniques than all of your competitors combined.

If you go about doing most of the things in this book now, you'll be on top of creating unique content, that is being shared across your target market, bringing back link juice, likes, hearts and most importantly bucket full of revenue back into your pocket.

Yes, this is hard work to set up but once completed you will have a business asset that will continue to generate sales for your business perpetually and with little effort!

Go & Dominate Your Market

Or

Visit www.lions.marketing, connect with me and I'll personally guide you to leveling up your digital marketing!

ABOUT THE AUTHOR

Founder of Lions Marketing (www.lions.marketing), Abdul Farooqi is best-selling author and outspoken authority on digital marketing practices. A graduate of UBC's Sauder School of Business, and formerly an Investment Banker, Abdul turned down his Wall Street ambitions and pivoted his analytical and business smarts to help small businesses jump-start their practices.

With his educational approach and fresh perspective on digital marketing, he soon became a go to resource for over a hundred dental practices all across North America. In addition, he serves as a marketing advisor for a number of large businesses, including CrisDental – one of the largest dental groups in Oregon as well as several venture backed start-ups.

Although Abdul talks, walks and dreams business growth (whether he wants to or not), he loves to travel & sink his teeth into all sorts of different cuisine. So far he's experimented with escargot in Canada, barbecued squirrel in Brazil, cow tongue with feet in Middle East, stewed camel meat in Pakistan, and, lobster marinara in Dominican. The animals are happy that he's usually busy working.

Made in the USA
Monee, IL
10 March 2021